I want to start this workbook by thanking all those who have chosen to walk this journey with me. For me this has been a very eye opening experience, not only writing this workbook and the book that accompanies it, but also going through the process that the Lord has taken me on. This book and workbook are just a small picture of what the Lord has shown me over the last few years on this subject. It is my prayer that as you read the book, and go through the workbook, that everything that Lord has revealed comes bursting through. I know that if you allow the Holy Spirit to guide you, he will lead you into all truth. Make sure to walk through this with an open heart and a made up mind in discovering the things of God.

Enjoy!

Introduction

BEFORE reading the introduction: How would you define modesty? Don't use Google to look it up, just come up with your definition from your own thoughts.

_____

_____

What played a part in your definition? In coming up with your definition, did you think of the clothes you or others wear? How did that influence your definition, if at all? Did you consider other aspects of modesty?

_____

_____

Do you think modesty matters why or why not?

_____

_____

Take a few minutes to draw a modest person vs an immodest person. Use the lines to add what makes them modest or immodest.

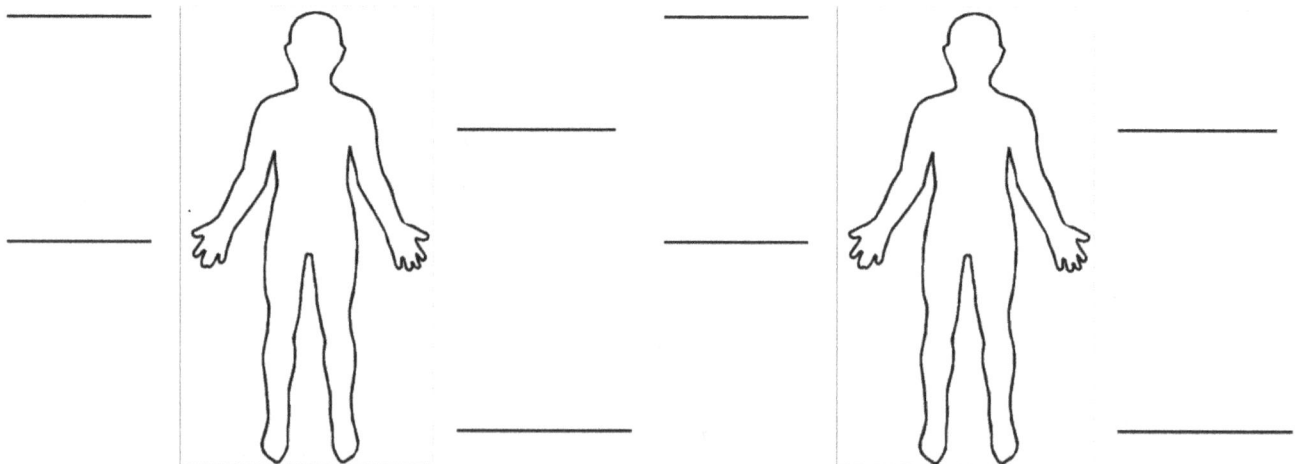

Begin by reading the Introduction of the book.

Chapter One

Chapter 1: Who Are You (No Really)

Read pages 8-10 (just the first paragraph of 10) then complete the activity
Use these lines to complete the WHO I AM task. Ask those around you who know you best if you are stuck. Refer to the list of descriptors in the book.

Who I Think I Am	Who I Am
_____	_____
_____	_____
_____	_____
_____	_____
_____	_____
_____	_____
_____	_____
_____	_____
_____	_____
_____	_____
_____	_____
_____	_____
_____	_____
_____	_____

Continue to read the rest of page 10 and the first paragraph of page 11.
Now take some time to cross off things from your list that speaks to what you have accomplished or acquired in some way. Don't worry we will come back to the second half of the list.

Then continue reading through this section of the book "Who Are You (No Really)".

<u>Molding the Clay</u>

Read pages 13-16 (the first paragraph).

Think about three moments that shaped how you view yourself. Explain how these moments affected you whether positively or negatively.

Shaping Moment #1

_____

_____

_____

_____

Shaping Moment #2

_____

_____

_____

_____

Shaping Moment #3

_____

_____

_____

_____

Read pages 16-20 (top of page) and complete the activity below.

Take the remaining words from the lists you completed on page 2 and write down the words that were put on you by others. These can be things that others have said or thought about you that have now become what you think of yourself. To identify this, think of the first time you thought of yourself a certain way and think of what influenced that.

Attributes Given to Me By Others
_____
_____
_____
_____
_____
_____
_____
_____
_____
_____
_____
_____
_____
_____

Continue reading through page 21 the "Molding the Clay".

The Matrix

Read through to page 25 and then complete the activity below.
In the space provided write down the three things; what you believe about yourself, the truth of God's word about that thing, and where they overlap.

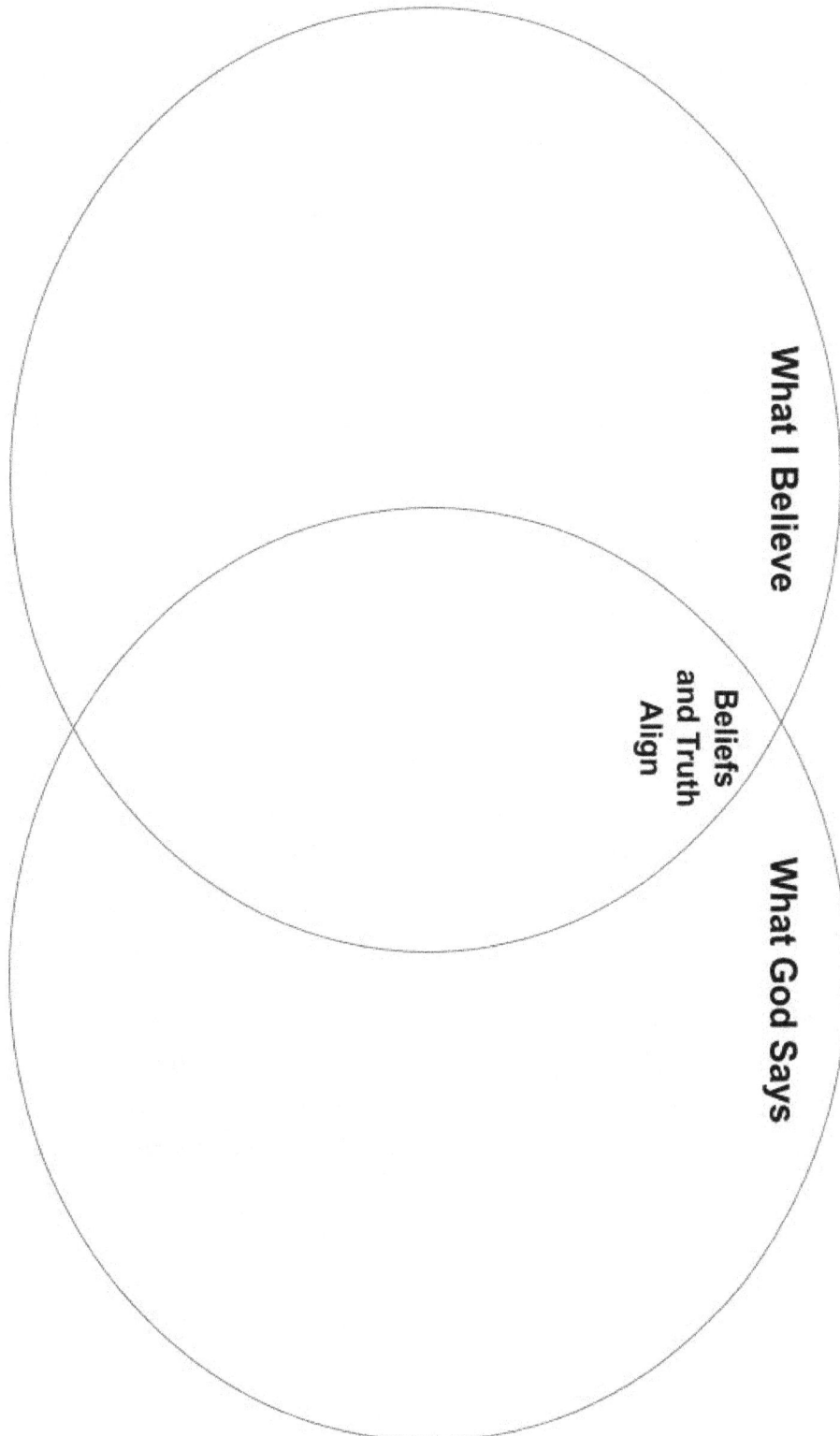

What I Believe

Beliefs and Truth Align

What God Says

Continue reading to the end of this chapter.

Chapter 1: Review

What have you learned so far in this chapter?

_____

_____

_____

_____

What ideas or thoughts of yourself has the Holy Spirit revealed that may not be accurate to who you really are?

_____

_____

_____

_____

As you continue in the book ask the Lord to further open up this subject to you in order for you to truly grasp all that you are in Him.

Prayer

Thank you Lord for the revelations you have already imparted through your word. I pray that you continue to show us your grace and mercy through revelations. Allow the Holy Spirit to open our eyes to what you would have for us to learn and help us to exchange our own thoughts and ideas for the truth of God's word. Thank you for all you have done.

In Jesus name, Amen

Chapter Two

Chapter 2: But What Does God Say?

Read to page 32 and complete the activity below. Write down what it means to be these things. I have given some examples from the book to help you, but feel free to add your own revelations from the word.

Who God Says I Am

Saved

_____

_____

Chosen

_____

_____

A New Creation

_____

_____

God's Tabernacle

_____

_____

_____

_____

_____

_____

_____

_____

_____

Continue reading through this section of the book to page 41.

Mosaic

Read through this section from page 42 to the beginning of page 48.

Think back through some of the moments in your life. Are there any moments where you saw yourself as broken, but later was able to see a glimmer of good through them? List any moments in your life where you could see that you were cut, but not broken. Give details of these moments and how you can see the cut versus brokenness.

Cut But Not Broken
•
•
•
•

Continue to the next section.

Challenge

Read to page 51 and complete the activity below.
By this time you should have completed 3 different lists; Who I Think I Am, Who I Am, and Who God Says I Am. Take all the words left on your lists and find scriptures to either confirm or deny these words, (this may take a while so if you need to come back to this after giving it some thought, thats fine).

Who I Am	Scripture	Confirm or Deny	
_____ →	_____	■	■
_____ →	_____	■	■
_____ →	_____	■	■
_____ →	_____	■	■
_____ →	_____	■	■
_____ →	_____	■	■
_____ →	_____	■	■
_____ →	_____	■	■
_____ →	_____	■	■
_____ →	_____	■	■
_____ →	_____	■	■
_____ →	_____	■	■
_____ →	_____	■	■
_____ →	_____	■	■

Continue to read the <u>Challenge</u> section

Is there anything stopping you from being able to see who you really are/seeing the truth of who you are? If so, think of what that could be and why.

_____

_____

_____

_____

_____

_____

_____

_____

_____

_____

Chapter 2: Review

What have you learned so far in this chapter?

_____

_____

_____

_____

What insights has the Lord given you thus far?

_____

_____

_____

_____

What ideas/thoughts have you had to challenge?

_____

_____

_____

_____

Prayer
Father God we thank you for all that you have shown us through your word. I ask that you continue to show us your wisdom and help us to challenge the views we have created in our lives and exchange them for your view of us.

In Jesus name, Amen

Chapter Three

Chapter 3: Modesty (No It's Not Just What You're Wearing)

BEFORE reading this chapter answer the question below.
How would you define a gentle and quiet spirit? What does it look like to have a gentle and quiet spirit?

_____

_____

_____

_____

_____

_____

It's All About Attitude

BEFORE reading this section, read 1 Peter 3: 1-4. What are your first impressions of this scripture?

1 Peter 3:1-4

Wives, in the same way submit yourselves to your own husbands so that, if any of them do not believe the word, they may be won over without words by the behavior of their wives, when they see the purity and reverence of your lives. Your beauty should not come from outward adornment, such as elaborate hairstyles and the wearing of gold jewelry or fine clothes. Rather, it should be that of your inner self, the unfading beauty of a gentle and quiet spirit, which is of great worth in God's sight

_____

_____

_____

_____

Continue reading through this section.

The Gentle Spirit

Read this section up to page 59.
Have you ever needed the gentle spirit of God? Describe a moment where God came to you as a gentle spirit. What did you learn about him. Do you think you would have learned the same lessons if he had come as a mighty fire or earthquake? Why or why not?

_____

_____

_____

_____

_____

_____

_____

_____

_____

_____

_____

_____

Continue reading the rest of this section.

What would a gentle spirit look like to you?

A Gentle Spirit is...

- _____
- _____
- _____
- _____
- _____
- _____
- _____
- _____

The Quiet Spirit

Read this section in its entirety.

Would you consider yourself as having a quiet/ stilled spirit or do you feel you have a more frazzled or restless spirit?

_____

_____

_____

_____

Ask yourself or those around you- what kind of interactions do others have when encountering me? When people talk to you what do they hear? If God heard your conversation and saw your interactions would he recognize you as his own?Why or why not?

_____

_____

_____

_____

_____

_____

_____

_____

What does a quiet spirit look like to you?

A Quiet Spirit is...

• _____

• _____

• _____

• _____

• _____

• _____

• _____

• _____

Modesty in Behavior

Read to the beginning of page 71, then answer the question below.

Have there ever been moments where your actions negatively impacted someone else? Think back to a time where you may have allowed your behavior to hinder others in some way. How do you know your actions negatively impacted others?

_____

_____

_____

_____

_____

_____

_____

_____

_____

_____

God calls us all to consider one another in all that we do. If you do remember times that you have not allowed modesty to shine through your behavior, pray this prayer with me and give God the room to work through your actions in changing your behavior to reflect his glory.

Father God I thank you for the revelation that you are pouring into my spirit at this moment. I pray that I am open to all that you have to show and teach me about behaving modestly. Help me to not only see the ways in which I may have been immodest but help me to change those things about me that have not shown my behavior as being modest.
In Jesus name I pray, Amen.

Sexual immorality and Impurity

Read the first paragraph in this section and answer the question below.
What do you think it means that sexual sins are the only ones committed against our own body?

_____

_____

_____

_____

Sexual immorality is a subject most people don't like to talk about but it is an important subject to cover as God mentioned it several times in the Bible. The act of sexuality immorality is so deep that satanists use it in their practice of worship. Understanding the depth of this can help us to see why God intended it for marital use only.

Read Genesis 19:1-25	Read Genesis 6: 1-7
What did the men do that solidified the wrath of God upon Sodom and Gomorrah?	What sinful acts were mentioned in this text that preceded God destroying the earth by a flood?
_____	_____
_____	_____
_____	_____
_____	_____
_____	_____

Let me be clear in both of these examples sexual immorality was not the only sin being committed. There were other depravities happening as well. But the evil that was seen in the Story of Sodom and Gomorrah and that was mentioned in the days of the flood were both dealing with sexual sins.
Continue to read the rest of this section to page 76.

Sexual sins can be very difficult to break. They have a tendency to take hold of our lives and spirits in ways no other sin does. If you find yourself struggling with this type of sin ask the Lord to begin the process of deliverance with you so that you can experience true freedom in this area of your life. Pray this prayer with me.

Lord God I thank you for showing me the areas of my life that have not conformed to your image. I pray that you release me from the power of these sexual sins and cleanse me of all impurities that have been committed whether knowingly or unknowingly. I surrender myself to you, for I know that your power is stronger than any sin, addiction or habit that may be trying to control me. I pray that all sexual immorality be removed from my life at this moment and never return by the power of the blood of Jesus. I thank you in advance for your deliverance over my life.

In Jesus name I pray, Amen.

Debauchery

BEFORE reading this section answer the question below.

How would you define debauchery? (yes you can use Google to help you)

_____

_____

Read the rest of this section then answer the questions below.

What is the difference between having a good time and engaging in debauchery? Where do you draw the line?

_____

_____

Think back to a time when you allowed yourself to overindulge in something. What led to that behavior? How did you notice that you were overindulging? What did you learn in that moment?

_____

_____

_____

_____

Lord, I thank you for showing me more about what debauchery is and how to combat it. I pray that you show me how to set boundaries for myself in order to be sure that I do not overindulge in the things of this world. I pray that you continue to open my eyes to see more of your revelations.

In Jesus name I pray, Amen.

Idolatry

BEFORE reading this section answer the question below.

What do you think of when you hear the word idolatry?

_____

_____

_____

_____

Are there any idols in your life that you can clearly see? Why do you think you have not surrendered these things to the Lord?

_____

_____

_____

Read this section to the end.

Do you think that there are areas of your life where you have become your own idol? If so, what are they?

_____

_____

_____

_____

What are some practical steps you can take to make sure that you are not making an idol of yourself?

_____

_____

_____

_____

We know that idolatry is a very serious thing to God as he does not share his place of glory with anyone or anything. Idolatry can look many different ways and it is important to make sure that you are open to hearing what the Lord is saying in this section and if you feel that there may be idols in your life you have not recognized or removed be sure to spend some time in prayer and ask the Lord to show these things to you.

Lord, thank you for opening my eyes to the things in my life that have tried to take the place that is set aside for you. Help me to rid myself of every idol, even if that idol is me. Help me to dethrone every area that is trying to exalt itself in my life. I pray that all idols are exposed and removed in this moment. Help me to make sure that nothing takes your place in my life.

In Jesus name I pray, Amen.

Witchcraft

BEFORE reading this section answer the question below.

What is witchcraft in your own words?

_____

_____

Read this section to the end.

All of us at some point have wanted or needed to control certain things in our lives. When do you think this idea borders on manipulation?

_____

_____

_____

_____

Have you ever found yourself serving God from a place of selfishness? How did the Lord reveal this to you? How did he go about changing this mindset for you?

_____

_____

_____

_____

_____

_____

I want to make sure that I point out that witchcraft is a very deep subject and it goes so much deeper than we have explored in this book. But for the subject at hand I am only focusing on one part of this subject. To that end, witchcraft takes different forms and versions of it can reside in a believer unnoticed until it is revealed to us. When that happens it is not an easy pill to swallow, but keep in mind that God does not only show us the areas in our lives that need to be dealt with but he also helps us remove those things. If you feel the Holy Spirit nudging you to examine this in your life, do not hesitate. The same God who shows you the enemies tactics also equips you to fight against them.

Lord, thank you for opening my eyes to the truth of this matter. I know that all truth comes from you and I rebuke and bind the enemy and every lie that he uses to try and ensnare me. I pray that you allow me to see the areas where I may have opened the door to witchcraft. I pray that those doors be closed and the enemy be removed right now in the name of Jesus. I know that you have called me to new levels of wisdom and understanding and I rebuke every seed of witchcraft in my life and pray that you help me to grow in my understanding of this subject so I can better fight in this battle.

In Jesus name I pray, Amen.

Hatred

Read through this section then answer the questions below.

When was the last time you experienced feelings of hatred? Who or what did you hate and why?

_____

_____

_____

_____

What did you do to turn around those thoughts of hatred?

_____

_____

_____

What made it easy or hard to give up hatred?

_____

_____

_____

When God shows us the hatred in our hearts he does so in order for us to see and root out that evil. Have you given God the opportunity to root out the evil of hatred in your heart or are there still some remnants left?

_____

_____

Review 1 John 3:14-15

14 We know that we have passed from death to life, because we love each other. Anyone who does not love remains in death.

15 Anyone who hates a brother or sister is a murderer, and you know that no murderer has eternal life residing in him.

Why do you think God mirrors hatred with murder? Why is hatred so bad?

_____

_____

_____

_____

Lord, I know you are a God who loves. Hatred is not something that should reside in your children and so I pray that you help me to make sure that it does not reside in me. I know there have been times when I have fallen short, but I thank you for your forgiveness and mercy in those moments. Help me to see beyond momentary circumstances and see people as you do. Help me to really love the way you do in order to ensure that hatred has no place in my heart.

In Jesus name I pray, Amen.

Discord, Dissension, Factions

Read this section to page 97.

Why do you think discord is one of the six things mentioned that God himself hates?

_____

_____

_____

Read through the rest of this section.

How do you usually react when someone comes to you about a problem with another person? Do you join in with the list of complaints or try to stay out of it as much as possible? Give an example of a time where you have done both. What were the results?

_____

_____

_____

_____

_____

_____

_____

_____

_____

If you had been one of the church members in the example on page 99, what would you have done? What would have been your response?

_____

_____

_____

_____

Lord, I know this is an area that you hate. I know that causing any kind of discord is not an act that a child of God should do. Even in knowing this, there have been times when I did not walk in wisdom and acted in wickedness in this area. I pray that you help me to notice when these moments arise so that I can better combat them. Help me to walk away from others when they begin to start strife. In doing this I can better show the love of Christ to those around me.

In Jesus name I pray, Amen.

Jealousy and Envy

BEFORE reading this section answer the question below.

What do you think the difference is between jealousy and envy?

_____

_____

_____

Continue to read the rest of this section then answer the question below.

Remember a time when you were jealous. How did this feeling change you or alter the way you reacted to people and situations?

_____

_____

_____

In the past how have you reacted to feelings of envy?

_____

_____

_____

Lord, I know you see my heart. You see where there have been moments of jealousy and envy in me. I thank you for showing me the revelation of this word and I pray that all traces of jealousy and envy be removed right now in Jesus name. I know that each person is precious to you and thus there is no reason for jealousy or envy to take place. Forgive me for dealing with these things.
In Jesus name I pray, Amen.

Fits of Rage

BEFORE reading this section answer the question below.

What would you say is the difference between anger and fits of rage?

_____

_____

_____

_____

Continue to read the rest of this section.

Have you ever experienced fits of rage? What did you notice about this feelings? How was it different from anger?

_____

_____

_____

_____

Do you typically give yourself a moment to calm down when angry or do you allow yourself to 'sit' in the anger? What can you do to change the way you react?

_____

_____

_____

_____

Lord, I know that the enemy is constantly trying to create a foothold in my life and fits of rage is one of the ways he does this. I pray that in moments where anger tries to creep in my heart and grow that your love, and mercy will abound and I will be able to see how the enemy is working in that moment. I pray that my eyes are open to his schemes and that you help me to remove the anger before it can grow into rage.
In Jesus name I pray, Amen.

Selfish Ambition

Read this section in its entirety.

When does ambition become selfish?

_____

_____

_____

_____

I want you to think about the desires you have for your life. While it is okay to want things for yourself I want you to consider how many of the things you desire are born out of a desire to elevate yourself? What are some of the desires that may be born out of self ambition?

_____

_____

_____

_____

Have you ever found yourself trying to place yourself above others? Explain any moment you can remember doing this in detail.

_____

_____

_____

_____

We can see this in all areas of life, at our jobs, schools, and even in church. What steps can you take when you notice yourself trying to elevate yourself instead of focusing on the will of God?

_____

_____

_____

_____

> *Lord, help me to take stock of the desires in my life. Help me to make sure that my desires are not born out of a place of self ambition but out of a desire to do your will in every area of my life. I know there is nothing wrong with having goals and wanting to achieve them but help me to be mindful of the moments these goals become selfish in nature, so that i can refocus my life for your purposes and not my own.*
>
> *In Jesus name I pray, Amen.*

Drunkenness and Revelries

BEFORE reading this section answer the questions below.

Do you think that as a Christian there are certain things we should not do? If so, what are those things and why should we not do them?

_____

_____

_____

_____

What are your personal beliefs on alcohol? What has shaped those beliefs? Are they influenced by the word of God?

_____

_____

_____

_____

Read to the end of the section, then answer the question below.

One of the benefits that we have as a believer is knowing that there is a bigger picture going on than what the natural eye can see. Knowing this we must be mindful of every situation we become a part of. The enemy is not going to stop trying to destroy you in any way he can. And thus we must be vigilant and sober minded at all times and that includes being mindful of where we go, what we partake in, and the company we keep.

Have you ever put yourself in a situation that you know you should not have? What encouraged you to put yourself in that situation? Were you able to see the error of your ways or did it take time?

_____

_____

_____

Lord, I know that you have not called us to live a boring life but help me to see when my so-called 'fun' goes too far. I know there are some things that are better for me not to do and others are fine but help me to see this through your lens not my own. My lens is filtered through my own experiences and ideas, but I pray that I see things through the word of God. Open my eyes to the truth and help me to see, understand, and live by it.

In Jesus name I pray, Amen.

Chapter 3: Review

What have you learned so far in this chapter?

_____

_____

_____

_____

What insights has the Lord given you thus far?

_____

_____

_____

_____

What ideas/thoughts have you had to challenge?

_____

_____

_____

_____

Prayer
Father God I thank you for giving me the opportunity to confront ideas, thoughts and mindsets that have not been pleasing to your sight. Help me to use this information to walk in modesty and live a life that honors your name.

In Jesus name, Amen

Chapter Four

Chapter 4: What Not To Wear

Delicious Steak Dinner

Read to the beginning of 122.

Take a moment to draw yourself. Draw yourself in your favorite outfit. The one that truly captures your personality the best. Then on the lines below explain what it is about this outfit that you like. What does it say about you? What image does it portray about your personality?

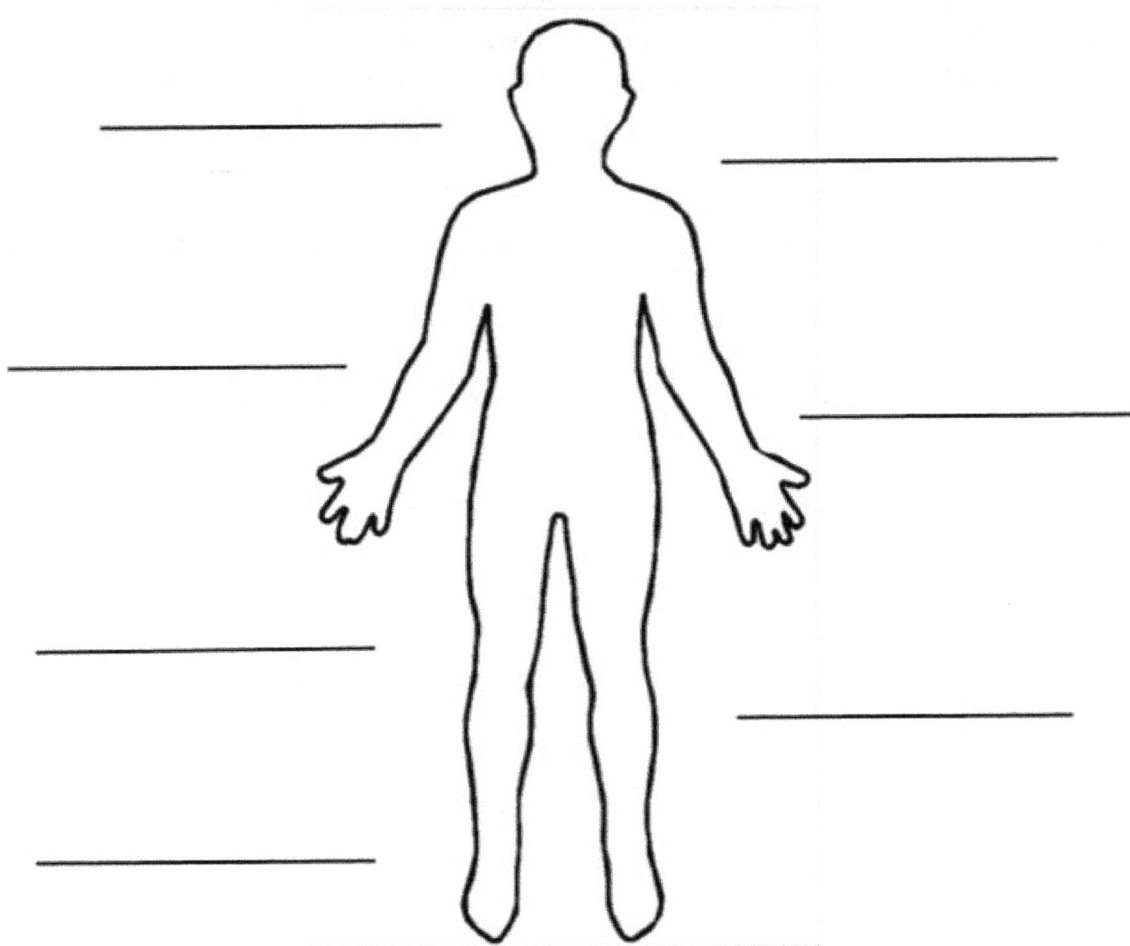

_____

_____

_____

_____

_____

_____

Read to the end of page 125.

What do you think it means that we are called to be the Temple of God?

_____

_____

Read to the end of this section.

If God were to come down and stand right in front of you wearing all the outfits you own, would there be anything you would feel the need to hide? Think about every outfit that you own and as you ask yourself this there may be a few outfits that immediately come to mind. I know that was the case for me in exploring this topic and no matter how I tried to maneuver my way around it there were a few outfits I simply could not justify. I then had to ask myself why I wanted to keep these outfits but the answer was always shrouded in vanity. So ask yourself the same questions and don't be afraid to really dig into this and allow the Lord to reveal those things to you.

_____

_____

_____

_____

The Temple

BEFORE reading this section, take a moment to jot down what you already know about the Temple/Tabernacle of the Old Testament. Whether that is how it's made, who made it or any other details that pop into your mind take this time to write them down.

_____

_____

_____

_____

_____

_____

_____

_____

_____

_____

_____

_____

_____

_____

_____

The Purpose of the Temple

BEFORE reading this section answer the question below.
What do you think was the purpose of the temple/ tabernacle in the Old Testament?

_____

_____

_____

_____

_____

_____

Read this section in its entirety.

What has changed or what have you added to your knowledge of the purpose of the Temple?

_____

_____

_____

_____

_____

_____

Building the Temple

Read through to the first paragraph on page 133.

Throughout this entire book we have been exploring areas of our lives where we are in need of a new outlook on ourselves. I know I have said this before but it bears repeating, it is important for you to be able to let go of anything that does ont align itself with who God has called you to be. In order to do that you have to sacrifice preconceived notions of yourself and every thought that does not match what God has said about you.

What are you carrying with you that may make it difficult for you to receive anything from God? In order to answer this question, take some time to ask yourself, 'What has been taking up my thoughts lately?' 'What thoughts or ideas have made it difficult for me to trust or believe in God?' 'Is there anything getting in the way of me embracing everything that God said I am?'

_____

_____

_____

_____

_____

_____

_____

Read the rest of this section in its entirety.

There is a difference between sacrificing (the brazen altar) and cleansing (the brazen laver). When I asked the Lord for more clarity on this he gave me this analogy. Let's say a person wants to quit smoking. They can sacrifice the act of smoking by removing the cigarettes from around them, by not buying them etc. But they will still have the taste for cigarettes in their mouth. Whenever they smell cigarettes their mouths will still fill with saliva with the desire to smoke. This is what needs to be cleansed and purified from them.
The cleansing process is not a one and done occurrence. Everytime the priests were to enter into the Holy Place they had to cleanse themselves. We know that our cleansing comes through the Holy Spirit who is continuously at work in us to help us purify ourselves and everything in us that is not like Christ. This idea moves into modesty as well. We know that there are aspects of this that may take time to really take root in our hearts and that's okay. List some things that you

can see God working on in your walk with modesty and how he has begun to work on those things.

What do you see God working on?	How do you see him working in that area?
1. _____	_____
	_____
2. _____	_____
	_____
3. _____	_____
	_____
4. _____	_____
	_____
5. _____	_____
	_____
6. _____	_____
	_____
7. _____	_____
	_____
8. _____	_____
	_____

The Holiness of the Temple

Read this section to the top of page 137.
After reading Leviticus 10:1-3 and 2 Samuel 6:6-7, what impression do you have of God? What gives you that impression?

_____

_____

_____

_____

Read to the middle of page 138. Read Leviticus 20:26.
We know that holiness is a very big topic. It is not one to be taken lightly but I want us to really start to think about what holiness looks like in our own lives. In describing you would anyone use the word holy? Why or why not?

_____

_____

_____

_____

_____

_____

Read through this section and answer the following questions.
What do your clothes currently say about you? Do they say you are a child of God or do they say you like to frequent the clubs? What about your clothes says these things?

_____

_____

_____

_____

Dating

Read to the end of page 141.

What ideas, thoughts of assumptions of yourself have you portrayed in your dating life? For some of us we may have to think back a while, but try and go back to that time and consider who you presented yourself to be.

_____

_____

_____

_____

What Should I Wear

Read this section in its entirety.

I want to point out that sexiness is not the only negative motivation when it comes to how we dress. Not everyone wants to be sexy. Some people just want to be seen. Now what i mean by this is that some people want to be the center of attention and so they dress in the most forward fashion clothes or the 'loudest outfits' they can find in order to make sure that they are noticed. This is another tactic of the enemy. Keep in mind he knows you very well and has been watching you since you were born. So he knows that for some people being cute, or sexy is not what they want. For others its simply being noticed. This can often result from issues with rejection of low self esteem, but the enemy knows this. So be sure to think on these things as well when considering your whats behind the way you dress.
When was the last time someone showed you attention? Think back to that moment. Why did that person suddenly notice you? Was it because of something positive or negative?

_____

_____

_____

_____

How Should I Act

Read this section in its entirety.

Think of the last time you were on a date or out with friends. I want you to really think about your behavior during that moment. Maybe for some of us on dates we get a little flirtatious. Maybe when hanging out with friends we may become the 'party animal' and get into excessive drinking and revelry. For some of us it may be easy to throw in a cute little wink at a stranger, or to drink more shots than our friends to show we can handle it. But these are real examples of our behavior not aligning with our calling.

What if God wanted you to minster to that stranger you were just winking at? What if one of those friends needed prayer to fight against alcoholism? Do you think they would feel they could come to you?

In this moment really take stock of your actions. What do they say about you? Do they say you areliving a modest and Godly life? Or do they show you as being just as lost of those in the world?

This may seem like an odd question but if we are really going to walk as children of God with his Spirit living inside of us then its one we need to consider. Take some time to really think about this.

_____

_____

_____

_____

_____

_____

_____

_____

_____

_____

What Should I Say

Read to the beginning of page 155.

Have you seen examples like this in your own life? When have you or those around you recognized the words they are saying do not align with the word and will of God? What made you realize this?

_____

_____

_____

_____

Read the rest of this section in its entirety.

Do others see a difference in you as a child of God? If you really took stock of your words and actions would they line up with who God says you are? If that is not the case what is stopping you from walking in who you are? Whether it be tradition, the desire to be liked, or simply wanting attention, what is stopping you from showing modesty in what you wear, how you act, or what you say? What can you do to help combat that?

_____

_____

_____

_____

_____

_____

_____

_____

All Tatted Up

BEFORE you begin reading.
What are your thoughts on tattoos? Do you have any tattoos? What was your motivation to get them? Would you recommend them to anyone else? Why or why not?

_____

_____

_____

_____

Read through to page 160. Then read Leviticus 19 in its entirety.
What are your thoughts on this chapter? Do you believe verse 28 is mandating the children of God to abstain from tattoos? Why or why not?

_____

_____

_____

_____

Read through this section to 164.
When you look at the world today where can you see the enemy trying to disfigure the image of God in his people both inside and out?

_____

_____

_____

_____

Chapter 4: Review

What have you learned so far in this chapter?

_____

_____

_____

_____

What insights has the Lord given you thus far?

_____

_____

_____

_____

What ideas/thoughts have you had to challenge?

_____

_____

_____

_____

Prayer
Father God I know that there are many areas of my life where modesty should be seen. I pray that you help me to see those places where I have not given you the room to do a work in me. Help me to better understand how to carry the principles of your word with me wherever I go. I pray I walk in the light of your revelation.
In Jesus name, Amen

Chapter Five

Chapter Five: Double Check

Read through this final chapter.

I want you to really take stock of all you have learned up to this moment. Though there may be some things you disagree with, make sure you are giving God the space to open your eyes to the truth of the matter. At the beginning of this book I asked the question 'Do you think modesty matters why or why not?' I want you to answer this question again but this time think of what we have discussed and see if your answer has changed.

_____

_____

_____

_____

_____

I pray that the Lord open your eyes to all that he is revealing in this moment. May every distraction, and demonic influence trying to rob you of the truth, be removed right in this moment. As we continue to walk in our life of modesty I pray that God remove the scales from our eyes and enlightens our hearts to his word in Jesus name, Amen.